War Stories

Antonia Hildebrand

War Stories
Poems for the Age of Fallibility

War Stories: Poems for the Age of Fallibility
ISBN 978 1 76041 448 1
Copyright © text Antonia Hildebrand 2017
Cover image: ragged hole in metal from bullets © Andrei Kukla

First published 2017 by
GINNINDERRA PRESS
PO Box 3461 Port Adelaide 5015
www.ginninderrapress.com.au

Contents

A Prisoner in the Garden	7
Haunted	8
Cutting Onions	10
The Shape of Things	12
Laughing in the Dark	15
Blood Moon	17
Where the Girl Jumped	18
Truth Has No Mouth	19
Small Mercies	20
War Memorial	22
Tour Guide	24
Stirring	28
School Photo	30
After Skimming	32
A Life in Three Parts: Junetown	34
The Alien Shore	38
Fairy Dust	41
The Wages of Hate	42
Gods in Space	43
Pity the US Soldier	44
When Artists Celebrate Virtue	45
The Beauty and the Crab	47
Plath On Plath	52
Afghanistan	54
The Our Gun	56
The Doll's Dream	57
Like a Hurricane	59
In Cold Blood	61
The Body Cannot Love	62
To a Murdered Child	64

Skinned Alive	65
Burning Pierrot	67
The Human Race Destroys Its Saviours	68
Collision	69
Red	70
True North	71

A Prisoner in the Garden

They couldn't say Mandela's name.
It was a charm,
an incantation.
When the press came to Robben Island
to see if it was really as bad
as all that,
a photographer captured Mandela
with his lens.
An angry black man
leaning on a rake, in his prisoner's uniform
his furious eyes masked by sunglasses,
on his head
a floppy cloth hat.
So armed, he stared the camera down.

They couldn't write Mandela's name.
It had power
and couldn't be made small.
not even pressed on to paper
in fine print.
So underneath the published photo
they put the weasel words,
A prisoner in the garden.

It's perfect.
Almost biblical.
As if he was in Eden,
and simply couldn't tear himself away.

Haunted

The time will come
when you would be glad
to see her ghost
so utterly is she gone.

Loss gives way to fear
shadows on a wall
take on a familiar shape.
An image like the after-image
on a retina
shivers there.

But this passes too.
Then there is nothing;
just a phone number
with no one at the other end
to answer.

Memories of a laugh,
a smile, her diamond eyes;
their exact shade of blue.
The way anger made her nose look sharp.
How empathy, in her, was almost ESP.

Love remains
but it has no target
and no recipient.
It floats on an emptiness that feels like vertigo.

Then fear goes too.
The shadows on the wall
are simply shadows.
Each cold thing is only what it is.

If her ghost came then
you would welcome it as an honoured guest
embrace vapour
and smile at her silence
as if she was only lost in thought.

Cutting Onions

I was cutting onions for the barbecue.
The onions prophesied to my eyes,
and they wept.
It was your birthday,
earlier I had given you a bottle of wine,
gift-wrapped.
But something was wrong.
The onions knew it,
my eyes knew it,
and soon I did too.

You had combed your hair to a point,
on top of your head.
You said it was funny and would make people laugh.
Is he crazy?
Or am I?
I didn't say it,
didn't even think it, then.
Nevertheless,
something was out of kilter.

Soon enough we were fighting.
I stood accused.
I was a ball breaker, like my mother.
Too pushy,
too predictable.
I had already opened the wine,
so I retaliated,
sinking steadily but firing all canon above the waterline.
The birthday was in tatters.
I felt hollow and sad and you raged,
with the pointy tuft of hair,
standing up on your head.
It was, I could see it now,
an act of defiance.
Let age come,
you would gore him to death,
with your hairy horn.
So you raged, and I wept.
The onions were right.

The Shape of Things

Hi-tech infantry
Smart weapons
Target of opportunity
Weapons of mass destruction
Surgical strike
Take out
The honour of serving in our common defence
Conventions of war
Rules of engagement
Human shields
Duration of conflict
Decisive conflict
Heightened state of alert
God bless our country
Shock and awe
George W. Bush
Bomb into submission
Saddam Hussein
Hit the bunker
Combat support operations
Missions
Early warning aircraft
Our fighting men and women
Deployed soldier
Action to disarm Iraq
Scuds
B52s
Cruise missiles

Main phase of the war
Anti-aircraft gun
Fluid situation
Chemical suit
Gas mask
Presidential palace
Tomahawk missile
Military planners
Stealth bombers
E bomb
Neutralise
MOAB
J dam
Daisy cutter
Small nuclear weapon
Coalition of the willing
In harm's way
Defence white paper
Massive attack

Red Sea
Gulf
John Winston Howard
Bunker busters
Penetrate
Biological weapons
Information overload
Prosecute an information war
Laser guided bombs
Small diameter bomb
Airborne troops
Ground battle

Electronic attack
Hostile country
Tony Blair
Special operations force
Significant impact
Basra
Fallujah
Oil wells
Allied war planes
The national interest
Unprecedented ferocity
New York Stock Exchange
Oil prices rise
Best little performer on the Dow
Defence stocks up.

Laughing in the Dark

It's easy to sit in the safety of the dark
and watch the blood fly.
Heads explode, hands are severed
Jack Nicholson does Jack Nicholson,
complete with Lucifer leer.

We sit in the dark in seats with headrests
as if the cinema will become airborne.
Oh how we laugh.
Loudly and uneasily.

A blonde, hands bound behind her
is shot execution style.
The gangsters laugh too.
She fell funny, one of them says.
Maybe, but we're not laughing.
Our popcorn catches in our throats.
But we laughed, later on,
when they shot the hit men.
We laughed when an undercover cop
had his broken arm pounded on a table.

We're not blonde, just female.
The empathy's not there.
It's true: she fell funny.
But there in the dark
we can only stare and gulp our scalding coffee.
Only right that we should feel some pain
feel something apart from the hysteria
of *Schadenfreude*,
the queasiness of shared guilt.

Later I remember the way a shadow
can cross open land on a sunny day.
The way a cloud can darken everything
in an instant.
The fragile existence described in 'To a Mouse'.
But Robbie Burns wasn't really talking about a mouse.
He was talking about Robbie Burns.

Blood Moon

Red moon at dusk
in a half-lit grey and orange sky

A blood moon
hanging from the elongated veils
of pink clouds,
that have been stretched by the wind
like molten glass.

Late at night
the wind still howls
and the world seems lost.
The past seems lost.

The lessons
(so hard to remember)
are unlearned.
The human race
is weary but defiant.
Unconvinced by history.
Unteachable,
and proud of it.

Where the Girl Jumped

Where the girl jumped,
smallish plastic shields like transparent wings,
meant to deter other jumpers,
have sprouted along the shiny, metal rails.

How she did it,
in the busy shopping centre,
is already legend.
One – she stood on the rail,
like a gymnast,
and then she just let herself fall.
Two – she didn't let herself fall,
it was a dare, someone dared her,
and she just fell.
Three – the people working in the shops downstairs,
saw her land – they all had to go home.
All these things are true,
since no one knows the truth.

What is unspoken,
is that in any crowd
there is always a potential jumper.
Someone almost broken,
frail as a torn kite,
wanting to fly;
but falling, falling.

Truth Has No Mouth

on the reign of John Howard

Truth has no mouth,
he's not sexy,
he's not fun.

He lives in a boarding house,
smells of age,
does not have friends in high places.
Truth bleeds,
is messy and inconvenient.
His cold comfort is simply that he knows what's true.

His only friend is the Word.
Truth's enemies hate the Word,
Almost as much as they hate him.
These two sit alone, together,
feared and scorned they struggle and strive.
They stay together, though.

Without the Word,
Truth would be silent.
And without Truth,
The Word would just be a noise.

Small Mercies

I go to the end of the hall,
look out from behind the curtains.
They make a pattern on my face.
Lace.
And sunlight.
As if I was tattooed.

There is no one there
and the garden is dry.
Do I dare go out and water it?
There is a man who wants to kill me.
>	I left him one hundred days ago.

I'll kill you, bitch
he told me as I went.
Casually.
He had always been
a casual kind of lover.

How was I to know he meant it?
That he would follow me from
town to town.
That he would try to strangle me,
in a rundown flat,
in a dusty little town
where I was hiding.

He had never been the
passionate kind.
But now he was.
The wild joy in his eyes
as he squeezed,
was the most animated
I had ever seen him.
His big hands brown and dry
from the construction site.

My screams made a neighbour
call the police.
I run.
I've been running ever since.
At night I shake,
sleep is as broken as my life.
In the morning I wake
and tell myself,
ironical to the last.
That was a day he didn't
kill me.

War Memorial

The statues never show the blood,
viscera hanging,
the eyes gone; or the head.
All neat and clean and symmetrical
heroes' names written in gold
tricks with light and shade
gardens of remembrance.

But those who were there
don't want to remember.
They say *lest we remember*,
but only when no one's around.
They march,
as once they marched off to war
When they were young and innocent.
No one speaks of the unspeakable,
it would be unpatriotic,
letting their dead mates down like that.
They allow the blood, the shit, the viscera
the frantic agonised grimaces,
the boys who screamed for their mothers
to fall, like teardrops
into the emptiness of time,
into silence.

Who would condemn them
for preferring the glint of sunlight on medals,
the optimistic sound of a marching band,
the street theatre of a parade?
Let the dead bury the dead
let the living mould themselves
to the myth of a demon race
that had to be destroyed.
A war to end all wars.
Of meeting again one sunny day.
The cheers of the crowd help them forget
it was their brothers and sisters they killed.
They march, haunted but smiling.
Afraid to remember, or to forget.

Tour Guide

Sixteen years I wandered there
among the ghosts.
The calculus of human lives, of dust,
of devilry, was laid open to me.
I knew every historical fact
worth knowing,
about people
I had never met.

The husband and father,
transported as a convict at fifteen,
for stealing a coat.
The wife with her thin, fragile face
and a slight overbite, arriving on the *Brilliant*
from Scotland.
(One of her babies had died in an upstairs
bedroom).
I wandered amongst
the detritus of their daily existence,
I read about his funeral procession
and his flair for optimistic plans.
But now I only see him in dreams.

I dreamed once that I was driving
past the building at night.
The lights were on and inside
a crowd of well-dressed people
were enjoying a violin recital.
I dreamed I had left jewellery in there,
on the counter.
Strange jewellery of an indeterminate blue.
I feared they would steal it.
Foolish to fear.
They had already stolen my life.

The building was Shangri-La in reverse:
I went in young and came out old.
But in the translation,
much was gained.
I understood at last
that human will and resilience
have their limits.
The husband overcame it all,
the homeless boy living on the streets
in England,
then put on the boat to Australia,
tainted with that inescapable convict past.

His funeral procession
was the biggest the district
had ever seen.
But, of course, he had moved
beyond all that.
He had moved to the inscrutable
one-way world of the dead.
But I see him in dreams,
red-haired and vigorous,
full of the vainglory of a pauper
grown rich.
And replete with a patient talent
for flattery of those who could
help him up the social scale.

So far away from the place
that gave such things meaning,
he could have the convict stain,
but also a fine house, horses and carriages,
even a maid.
It all ended in dust and death,
even though their furniture,
preserved like treasure from a
Pharaoh's tomb,
lived on.
As did the heavy, rusty little irons they used
to press ruffled petticoats and hooped skirts.
Only used as door stops now.
Celebrating the dead is a worthy thing.
But they are dead.
And all their dreams and sins
are with them in the grave,
where the thief and the statesman
share a fine democracy.

Stirring

Standing at the stove stirring
something in a pot,
you remember all the things
he's ever said to you
and about you in front of others.
Steam drifts up and memories rise with it.
But you don't rise.
You just stand stirring

as you remember every injury
every cruel, unjust word.
What comes is not hate
not even anger.
What comes is bitter contempt
for yourself.
Because you don't leave him.

Hobbled by self-disgust
and half-believing he is right
you stir and stir.
You stay right there.
You're trapped now:
all those contemptuous words
are wrapped around your heart
and your mind like chains.
Every taunt, every crazy accusation
glimmers in the steam, like a silver cup,
a trophy.
Like the ones he has from golf.

He set out to break you –
and he did.
You stir his food, set two places
at the table and stay right there.
The breadwinner must eat.

School Photo

I pose for the camera.
My hair is in plaits,
tied with ribbons in the school colours.
The new uniform is scratchy
on my five year old skin.
Shiny new shoes.
Grey socks.

I stand and pose and my uncle,
the photographer,
takes the photo.
First ever day at school.

About to be pushed, like a boat,
into the stream of life,
my plump little hands rest on my thighs.
Untrained and uninstructed,
I pose like a model.

I'm happy.
I love books, I want to go to school.
But when I look at my mother,
she seems lost.
Torn between pride and sorrow.

I wouldn't learn that lesson for many years.
It wasn't taught at school.
It was learned watching my own child race into school,
without a backward glance.
There is no photo.
Only me on the footpath, not leaving,
while parents mill around me.
Feeling what my mother felt.
A hand around my heart,
squeezing, squeezing.

After Skimming

written on Remembrance Day

I used to sleep so easily
everything was easy once.
Now just staying on my feet is a prize fight
with discouragement shouted from the sidelines.

Christmas was unmarred perfection
everyone I loved was there
and I ran from dawn to dusk
carrying delicious food in beautiful dishes.
Each dish held something
more delectable than the last.
Each gift (there were so many)
was an adventure
and I took each one for granted.

Now life is harder
sometimes lonely
and my body is beginning to let me down.

Should I complain?
I have had the best of it.
Been fortunate, been loved.
And blessed with the wisdom
to know love when I see it.

I no longer skim above the day
like a bird in flight
but I still have the memory
of leaving the ground.
Of flying.

Each sunset is still beautiful to behold
each morning a state of grace.
Full of anticipation,
I have never lost the sense
that anything at all can happen.
I felt as a child that each day was mine
to shape and steer.
I still do.

A Life in Three Parts: Junetown

I Size Two Shoes

The town I live in was your town.
One you came to as an exile after your father died.
You were the youngest and your mother bought you
Ballet shoes so you could dance around
on tippy-toe in the backyard at Roma.

There was nothing sinister, nothing that would justify
a long, sad memoir.
No sensational tragedy, no secret past.
You just went to boarding school there,
never knowing as you sang Ave Maria to the nuns
in that virginal soprano,
that you would give birth to eleven babies in
this town.
A snobby, cliquey place,
full of intrigues and incomprehensible crimes.
Underneath the neat streets and pretty gardens,
something angry and wayward loitered –
as perhaps it always does.
In any town.

By sheer chance our War Service house,
ended up in the better part of town,
as the long dirt road up a hill close by became bitumen,
and the invisible markers of social class went up.
This accidental status was never reflected
in the family's bank balance,
but you went to the movies and to coffee and to choir,
and to church,
in your pretty clothes and tasteful jewellery,
as if it was.
You were proud of your tiny feet,
'Size two,' you would say,
holding them out to be admired.

When we emptied the house to sell it,
after you died,
we found a tiny black leather baby shoe
of mine, in a drawer.
You had kept it all those years,
proud that your baby girl had inherited
your small feet.
Now the shoe sits on a bookcase,
with a family tree of photos.
It seems symbolic;
of your pale and freckled feet,
and the elegant little shoes you wore.

Always busy.
Always going somewhere,
walking quickly.
Eager as a child, even into old age,
for what lay around the corner.

II Piano Playing

She's the reason I can never hear a piano playing
without hearing it as if it was playing in the next room.
Near, near to me, close to my heart.
She's what makes me feel, still,
 a frisson of fear when I smell beer,
her fear of drunkenness as near to me as if it was my own.
Her thoughts tame mine.
I believe people can be too rich and too thin.
I believe the rich are to be despised and envied
simultaneously, and that to fail your children is to fail utterly.
Songs my mother taught me.
She loved me first and best.
This is the family romance: so they tell us.
Maybe.
Perhaps my mother made love too important,
But how could that be done?
And by whom?
The tinkling notes die away.
The heart and the mind tick over.
The tinkling notes of an old fashioned song
settle on the air.
Fatal, but not serious.

III Birthday by the River Styx

Death is as natural as breathing,
but this is not natural,
my mother's last birthday celebration.
She is dying of cancer,
worried by death,
as if a dog had her in its hairy jaws.
So thin and so frightened,
even under the opiates.
At night she can't be alone.
The dark is death's brother,
and she notices the resemblance.
But this winter's day,
there is wine,
apple pie and cream, lasagne,
a birthday cake, bunches of roses.
All her children are there,
Ray Charles is on the CD player singing,
'I Can't Stop Loving you',
with that smoky catch in his voice.
And it's true.
I can't.

The Alien Shore

dedicated to Hugh Bradshaw, a soldier of that war

The waves breaking on the alien shore
were strangely gentle.
Nothing like Bondi.
Later, at home your mind, breaking,
and the electric shock treatment.
The clarity of that furtive jungle battle
where everything crystallized into that moment
when the bayonet pierced your flesh.

The fervent, muddy, rain-soaked embrace
of the New Guinea jungle
from which you feared you would never escape.
Some of them were only boys.
Working in an office one day,
in a uniform training with wooden guns the next.
Budgets didn't stretch to training with real guns.
At night hiding, sweating and exhausted
under a cloud covered moon.
Grateful for the darkness,
protection from the Japanese snipers.

The muddy jungle tracks all looked the same.
Roads to bloody, silent struggles
where throats were cut.
And a single shot ringing out
from the tree tops saw another soldier fall,
to be dragged up out of the mud.
Cigarettes shared in the stifling humidity.
The knowledge always there,
enormous, crushing,
that if you failed,
Australia could be taken and occupied.

Knowing that the Japanese despised surrender.
The choices left were fight, kill or be killed.
Back home, years later,
your pretty little nieces would look at you
with innocent eyes.
Wondering why you were so silent, so withdrawn.
Making you smile, even laugh
with their foolish joy.
They didn't know.
But you had fought so they didn't have to know.
And that was good enough.
Almost a panacea for what you had endured
on the alien shore.

What was broken would never mend.
So you smoked your pipe near the wood stove,
In your sister's house.
A loved and respected man who never married.
And knew with rare certainty that joy,
now, for you,
was their joy.
Their safety.

Fairy Dust

It lies on its side
perfect and perfectly dead.
covered in the dust the bombing left.
You could call it a fairy baby,
covered in fairy dust,
only sleeping.
Tell a story a child could understand.
Because no child would comprehend
the truth of why that baby died.

The monstrousness of it
would be beyond them.
They would never understand
that those who killed it
are already telling themselves
it had to be done.
Drinking a postprandial whisky
in Washington.
Musing on the imperial burden
as their kind always do.

Another baby left Syria
in its terrified mother's arms.
They have taken on the stigma
of the refugee.
Unwanted, feared – even hated.
While in a parallel universe,
the whisky drinkers tell
their childish tales,
and play their bloody game
of chess.

The Wages of Hate

It's easy to see why some people call her a 'thing'.
The wooden-looking face, unpolluted
by a scintilla of intelligence.
The eyes so cold and blue
they seem to be made of glass.
The artificial clown-red hair,
the tinny voice like a record played
on a wind-up gramophone.

A voice that can only spew lies
as if Hitler was in drag
and giving one of his mad, incoherent speeches
to the gullible.

There she stands in the parliament,
only made relevant by hate.
For giving a voice to the vicious and the misled,
she is paid , not thirty pieces of silver,
but a quarter of a million dollars a year.
The wages of hate.
And for Manmeet Alisher the wages of hate
were also high.
He paid with his life, on his bus.
Murdered at his ordinary job, on an ordinary day.
Meanwhile, we democratically elect a fool,
so that we can all feel safe.

Gods in Space

They float up there in space,
dressed like beings from another world.
Which they are.

Why do they smile that way on the news?
Is it a nervous tic?
A rictus of fear?
Or a deluded feeling of escape from being human?

They are superpeople in space.
Lighter than air.
Even their shit floats away
if they don't follow Procedure.

Like helmeted angels they fly from button to lever
and back again.
Their backdrop is the universe,
dark and twinkling.
But down here on earth they are not weightless.
And they bring no new enlightenment back
to share with humanity.

Instead their work helps their masters
to put weapons into space.
So that, this is their mad delusion,
they can zap the bad guys from on high.

Star warriors.
Gods who kill.
But only, of course, for all the right reasons.

Pity the US Soldier

Pity the US soldier,
A pawn in someone else's
Lawrentian fantasy of a band of brothers.
Fighting for a cause that is a lie.
A cause he doesn't even understand.
He joined the army to have a job,
get health insurance,
or an education.

Sometimes his wife and child are far away.
Sometimes his wife is a soldier too.
Sometimes his child has followed
in his blood-stained footsteps.

High flown dreams of valour
if he ever had them,
became a nightmare of mangled bodies,
sudden death,
adrenaline and nervous shock.
But not amnesia.
not that longed-for grace.

Obey.
Conform.
Kill.
These things are hard to unlearn,
and all the evil in the world
comes from one or other of them.

Better far to cry *non serviam*
and fall from what the world sees as grace.
Better to be Lucifer
than a cipher.

When Artists Celebrate Virtue

When artists celebrate virtue
we turn away with a knowing smile.
It hurts us in some way,
to see virtue paraded.
To see the loving mother with her child.
Is it because we think God is dead?

Well, yes, we say,
We know all that.
She is known.
She loved us.

But, in fact,
we know there was more.
A hidden affair,
A child born in secret,
given away.
Depressive episodes.
An attachment to the sherry bottle.

And then there are those who were raised
by genuine female monsters,
mothers who would give Medusa a run for her money.
People like that don't turn away.
they have hearts clogged with scar tissue,
and veiled, mocking eyes.
They've been turned to stone.
They study mother and child very carefully,
with a soft, serial-killer smile.

We want to believe in the light,
but for most of us the dark
is more credible.
Even though virtue is a fact:
without it human existence would not be possible.

All in all, though
the poets get it right.
Born half to rise and half to fall.
A piece of work-in-progress
in which light and shade are always at war.
Virtue is never all of it.

We want the whole story:
dread that they will tell it.

The Beauty and the Crab

I

When we went to the beach as children,
crabs were comical.
Blue soldier crabs marching
sideways across the sand.
Disappearing into holes.
While the ocean, the ceaseless ocean,
rolled and sparkled.
We laughed at them.
We chased them,
our hair whipped by the wind.

But now time chases us,
and the crab is more a *bête noire*.
First our mother, carried off in its claws,
fighting with the heart of a lion.
Her fight as ceaseless as the sea.
And then finally taken.
Gone.
Only a fragile doll remained in
the hospital bed.

The crab has no reason to spare us,
we do not spare him.
He is consumed by us
and sometimes as we age,
we are consumed by him.
Nothing buys him off.
Not beauty, not talent, not wealth.
We cannot make a deal.

II

A sister's voice on the phone,
Have you spoken to Maryann lately?
No.
She's got a tumour on her thyroid.
It's malignant.
Impossible.
My beautiful, talented sister?
The artist, the powerhouse,
so gifted and unique?
Not her.
It couldn't be.
But I knew it was.
The tests.
The scans.
The hope.
M for Monday.
M for MRI.

I had vaguely thought,
not being one to dwell on such things,
that we would go on,
tottering down Oxford Street in Bulimba,
invading bookshops and coffee shops,
cackling over nonsense until well into
our dotage.
Was that now not to be?
No one really knew.

But it was chilling to hear
that they had told her,
We might have to take your voice box.
She told them, no.
You'll have to find another way.
A nightmare, unrolling like a bolt
of black cloth and spilling across our lives.
An endoscopy left her face and throat in pain.
A mere dress rehearsal.

III

In a bookshop in Oxford Street,
we once found a book called,
The Selfish Genius.
With an impish grin, she said,
A book about you!
I was too surprised to reply.
Did she really see me that way?
I can still remember the feeling
that an abyss had opened at my feet,
when she said, quite stoically,
We have to hope the radiation
And the chemotherapy work,
They can't operate.
We were in the lobby of a cinema
in Brunswick Street.
And the traffic outside,
the faces of the pedestrians,
the trees,
the old cinema itself,
all seemed as unreal as a film set.

As unreal as the thought
she could die.
All we have is hope.
The fragile courage of the conscripted.

IV

A group email arrives from her
hospital bed.
She has heard that we are worried,
but she is fine.
Even though she's a public patient,
she's scored a private room
with a kitchenette and her own fridge.
The food is fabulous.
She has a new laptop
and Netflix to watch.
There is a chapel where she can pray,
and attend mass.
She even has a bottle of Sav Blanc
in her fridge.
She will be home for Christmas and
she's very happy about that.
It ends, 'Love to all'.
She is exhibiting the same
heart of a lion as our mother.
Secretly we hope that's where
the similarity ends.

And then the emails, the phone calls,
facebook, all stop.
You retreat into the nausea of chemo,
the pain of radiation burns and silence.
Unbidden, there's that line from
'Sounds of Silence',
'Hello darkness, my old friend'.
Then a pirouette away from THAT.
Not yet, not yet.

V

Finally, one ordinary morning
she gets an extraordinary call.
I've got terrific news, the doctor says,
handing her back her life.
It's completely gone.
Her nemesis is no more.
The suffering she endured
has been her salvation after all.
She looks out the window and
notices how lush and green the grass is.
That amazing green floods her eyes,
her senses, her very soul.
Drizzly rain begins to fall.
Dry-eyed she watches it and
reaches for the phone.

Plath On Plath

Sometimes I battened my talent down,
like a woman hiding a pregnancy.
But in that cold house where I could see
the breath in front of my face,
Ariel demanded to be born.
And in the blue mood of early morning
my children sleeping in another room,
I communed with my disquieting muse.
My golem,
so cunning, so full of trickery.

A volcano of poetry erupted,
and she sucked me down
into the dizzying red of creation.
My clever Thought Fox had been cheating,
Eating my excellent cooking,
calling his mistress on the phone,
While I built my false Nirvana.
New baby, end of marriage.
I was losing my milk,
feared I would lose my mind.

This world made a meal of me,
but I triumphed anyway.
Cooked the books,
gave the world a bellyache.
I was a witch by then,
living on air.

The icy glitter of my despair,
caught the light on the way down.
Poem after poem spilling on to the page,
waiting in my study like unexploded bombs,
while I lay my head on a towel in the oven,
(so clean, so industrious, so efficient),
and the gas filled my lungs.
It was a scientific decision;
science always made me panic.
It reminded me of my father.

The moon looked down,
wearing her hood of bone.
She gave no sign and I, myself,
had never expected help from that
quarter.
Later the Thought Fox tore some
pages out of my journals.
I should have burned them.
Eaten the ashes.
I killed the Good Girl,
in that freezing house;
left my children cups of milk.
Then I left my body and travelled down to
the sea floor,
where my crippled father lived.
The tall girl who swam out to sea
but could not drown,
was breathing water at last.
Under a shimmering, seaweed sky.

Afghanistan

'I will not kiss your effing flag.' – e.e. cummings

Denied God by philosophers and scientists
we build cathedrals of bones, piling them up
like medieval builders,
devout and wedded to a task
that may take centuries.

But we're not like them. We don't believe.
We do it out of habit…

Modern warfare still mimics the dead airman
in *Lord of the Flies*: there seems to be
purposeful movement – then we see it has
maggots for eyes, and from its mouth
comes a tinny, disembodied voice
like the sound of dusty gramophones
playing to themselves in empty rooms
eerie with irrelevance.

                         …an old photo:
my six year old daughter sits on a couch
holding her baby brother on her lap.
Now that she is woman and he is man,
what does my generation leave them?
Pax Americana or whirlwind?

              the thought comes that
war is a bone scan, strips us to the bone
shows us what we are made of…but no
that would be something comprehensible
black patch on a bone – name the disease,
name the cure…

War is simply a frame for our unoriginal sins.
Murder. Rape. Theft.
All paths lead to the grinning death's head
we become.
No diagnosis there, certainly no cure.

Even the smiling torturers,
flashing v signs at the camera,
follow in the footsteps of other torturers.
Follow the razzle-dazzle
of monuments and medals.
To put it crudely,
in a torture chamber there is no eureka moment
the human body defines the work, and defies
innovation.
The wickedly efficient technology
for which they have a strange love
delivers the same old creed.
If you prick us, we bleed.
And The Other has been given
 yet another face,
so we can be tricked into thinking that we know
who will come for us in the night.

The Our Gun

Our gun who art in heaven
hallowed be thy calibre.
Thy kingdom come
thy kill be done
in the mall as it is in the car park.

Give us this day a thousand rounds
and forgive us our misses.
Deliver us to homicide
and lead us into evil.
Amen.

The Doll's Dream

The doll sits in her china doll glory
on a dresser near the window.
In an old house in an old street.
The little girl has grown up and left.
She is a big success,
and works in a tall building in the city.
Everything they ever wanted for her
came to pass.

One night the girl who is a success goes to bed
and dreams that the china doll is dreaming.
The doll dreams of the past,
sitting on the antique dresser.
In her dream she is wrapped again
in the girl's arms, while she sleeps.
The doll dreams of hearing the little girl's
wispy breaths.
Feeling her warmth.

In the dream she can speak.
She is whispering to the little girl:
we don't need much,
you and I.
Give me back what was taken away,
and we will both be happy again.
Then the doll's voice fades,
and the dreaming girl can only hear a faint, metallic rustling,
like Christmas decorations being taken down.

She wakes, feeling
a sadness she can't name,
smokes a cigarette and forgets what she dreamed.
In another house far away,
the doll waits near the window,
its pretty face frozen in a smile.

Like a Hurricane

I put the CD on.
Carefully.
This is my current addiction, discovered
while looking for another song.
Neil Young.
You are just a dreamer, he sings,
in that innocent, broken voice.
He sings about a girl who's walking
from star to star,
and how he's getting' blown away.
But it's me: I'm blown away.

Then a half-mad angel starts
tearing into an electric guitar.
Don't know his name, don't want to know.
For this virtuoso turn mystery seems somehow to be required.
And it reminds me of Germany,
and the first time I heard Carly Simon
singing 'No Secrets'.
(The particular, dangerous enchantment of the words she sang.)
Of making love in the Blue Mountains,
of being drunk and being kissed leaning up against
the wall of a pub in Germany: it had seen it all before.

Howls break from the keening guitar,
great cosmic swoops,
the way a heart would sound if it could make music.
Time stops but the song still ends,
with that deep, fat chord.
I take the CD off,
put it back in the plastic case,
leave it in a drawer.
Hidden.
Like heroin.
Like lust.
Like the stab of losing things you thought you wanted.

The song puts on no airs,
but it knows a trick or two.
Dark gold lighting in a bottle,
shooting me in the heart.

In Cold Blood

Murder most foul.
The rolling silver coin
and the faulty latch.
How well he understood.
Truman Capote had a miserable childhood.
Abandoned by his drunken mother,
the dark found him early.
It became familiar: the only certainty.
After I read *In Cold Blood*
I didn't sleep for weeks.
The little monster/master
had taken away my Catholic universe
of sin and sanctity
and given me another.
A universe of random acts
that were, in fact, no more
random
than the paths of the planets.
Evil now came in shades of grey.
And I suddenly found the darkness
and silence of night
unendurable.
I told one of my sisters about this once.
She nodded.
she hadn't slept for weeks
either
after reading the book.
It was like sharing a guilty secret.
But why did we feel guilty?
Capote sold his soul:
took ours instead

The Body Cannot Love

The body cannot love.
Only a fool would say I love with all my heart,
might as well say with all my shoulder.
The body lies,
even to itself with blushes, sighs and
palpitations,
that mean no more than a belly ache,
after an over-spiced meal.
Love comes from somewhere else,
entirely.
Perhaps it comes from a star,
or from another planet.
It's rarely found on this one.
Love doesn't live in the body,
if it did,
we'd cut some of it off,
every time we cut our fingernails,
we'd lose it with our sweat.
Love lives in the tinder box of our souls,
as frail and strange as the moth
Robert Frost saw on a snowy,
bone-cold day.

It perched on his hand,
and he talked to it,
(as a poet naturally would).
Then it fluttered off to certain death.
Frost wrote a poem about it,
preserving the life he couldn't save.
Why did Frost care?
Simply put, it was love he saw
on the wing that day.
Mysterious and doomed.
We've all been lost in the cold.
Ask the prostitute,
ask the ravished child,
Ask the hunter sucking marrow
from a bone.
The body cannot love.

To a Murdered Child

Your sweet mouth closed on something bitter.
You wanted to love- even what hurt you.
Innocent eyes, glossy dark hair,
your little white teeth bared
in a pretty smile.
Who can you trust now?
When you make your way into
the Underworld,
who will hold your hand?
When the sinless die violently,
where do they go?

I see you sometimes,
on a sunny day;
floating in the light,
just above eye level,
Like a filament from the gauzy,
exploding head of a thistle.
Slowly becoming something lost and perfect.

Skinned Alive

So is the creature flayed,
Beginning with the head.
Everything begins with the head.
Thrust head-first into the world,
then diving out of it head-first,
a frightened thing,
trying to hide its selves in the void,
the emptiness of space,
making a heaven out of necessity.

The layers peel away,
until the consciousness hangs in strips,
hangs by a thread.
The blood, the sinews, the electrics,
pulse and snap.
and send the pain,
like a telegram bearing bad news.
The unhinged cry slowly echoes.

So is the creature flayed;
and truth emerges.
But truth is not always rational.
Clearly the meaning (such as it is) is there.
I carry it in every cell,
but I still see it eluding me out of
the corner of my eye.
It is a game devised by a cunning lunatic?
Is it a test, the flaying pain of consciousness?

The meaning distorts and wavers,
I cannot hold it clearly in my sight.
What remains is fear.
Fear that all this darkness will follow us,
even into the void.

Burning Pierrot

At sunset,
Pierrot appeared, aflame.
Towering over some darkish trees,
amongst flaring, vermilion clouds.
His ruff was charred,
but he had dignity,
and he seemed to be thinking.

The rest of the company,
discussed the irony of it.
Punchinello, Columbine and the others.
Pierrot and his pale, painted face.
a fool for love, indeed.
Hanging himself on a silken cord.
Ruining the season.

He was always so silent, mused Columbine,
as they all stared into the sunset.
I don't think we can really say we knew him at all,
said Punchinello, with a sigh,
turning his best profile to the others.

Then they spoke of other things.

But when they closed their eyes,
Pierrot was there.
Pathos, or perhaps the sunset,
had burned him into their retinas.
Charred ruff, silken cord, painted face and all.

The Human Race Destroys Its Saviours

No one can explain it.

They crucified Jesus,
shot John Lennon,
who said his band was more popular than Jesus.
They killed Spartacus in battle,
burned Joan of Arc,
beheaded Thomas More,
sent him to Erehwon.

Socrates was forced to drink hemlock,
for no other crime than that of being
outrageously wise and clever.
Raoul Wallenstein saved thousands of Jews
from the Nazis.
Murdered by the Russians, they say.

Poor Dr Semmelweisz.
brilliant enough to discover bacteria,
and to tell doctors to wash their hands.
Not wise enough, however,
to ignore their taunts,
their whispered laughter and the way
they went on killing newly-delivered women.
He went mad.
Died in a lunatic asylum.

Four legs good, two legs bad,
or any other barbaric nonsense
that comes to mind.

No one can explain it.

Collision

The words crash and burn;
nothing scans.
I cross them out.
Put them in coffins.

I know the words
will eventually do what I want.
I just have to wait on the muse.

So I put the notebook aside.
Drink coffee.
Listen to Neil Young and Crowded House.
Put food out for the birds.

I wait,
humming,
like a car that wants to race.
Wait for the moment
when I can dip the pen
in my veins,
write with the blood.

Red

The red of love
is the tip of a flame.
Not like the red of war
with its bloodied corpses,
bombs, noise and grief.

Not like the red of hate.
The distorted face,
the bulging veins,
the clenched fists.

Not the red of cruelty.
Not the red of shame.
It is the red of the hibiscus,
the red of wine,
the red of a sun at sunset.
It is the scarlet that burns your eyes.

As Omar Khayyam wrote,
The day on which you are
without passionate love
is the most wasted day of your life.

True North

Iron clings to a magnet.
Metal filings fly through air
to embrace it.
So I cling to you and fly to you.
Forces that I don't understand draw me.
I who love freedom,
have none.

To find my way,
I must know the difference
between magnetic north and true north.
True north is aligned to the North Pole
and is constant.
Something to believe in when
all the gods have failed,
or gone away.

West – watch the sunset
and you're facing west.
South – face the sun at midday
and you are facing south.
East – standing at dawn facing
the rising sun you are looking east.
North – point to the left,
while watching the sun rise
and you are pointing north.

There's a scientific reason,
I'm sure,
for why I turn in your direction.
Why I orbit you like a moon.
North, east, south and west all lead to you.
So there is no difference,
whatever the compass says.

But the compass prevents shipwreck,
and there have I been, too often.
True north, the other north, is essential
for navigation.
For the precise line that takes you
where you want to go.

While love is a mystery that lies,
even to itself,
true north is as true as any fact.
Truer than most.
And constant.
The fidelity of its calculation
is unwavering.
While that of the human heart is fatally fickle,
and only true to itself.

www.ingramcontent.com/pod-product-compliance
Lightning Source LLC
Chambersburg PA
CBHW062153100526
44589CB00014B/1823